ST MARY MAGDALENE

SANDRINGHAM CHURCH

The little church of St Mary Magdalene is on The Queen's private estate at Sandringham, and this short history is published by gracious permission of Her Majesty.

RIGHT: *One of the fourteen beautifully carved angels in the choir of the church.*

FACING PAGE: *The church in 1856, before King Edward VII bought Sandringham. The wall is no longer there.*

BACK COVER: *The lychgate used by Her Majesty The Queen, members of the Royal Family, and the general public who wish to visit and attend the services of Sandringham Church.*

SANDRINGHAM CHURCH

The Reverend Patrick Ashton

THE first Rector of Sandringham of whom we have record was Robertus Algar de Akenham, who was appointed in 1321 by his patron, the Prior of Westacre. So for many hundreds of years there has been a Parish Church here, though the present building is of a later date. Few records seem to have been kept, though it seems probable it was entirely rebuilt in the 16th century by William Cobbes, whose brass is now fixed to a large slab let into the east wall of the porch.

It was extensively restored by Lady Harriette Cowper in 1855 in memory of her only child, Marie Harriette, who had died tragically of cholera the previous year at Dieppe, aged two years. In 1861 King Edward VII, then Prince of Wales, bought the Sandringham estate from Lady Harriette's husband, the Hon. Charles Spencer Cowper, and in 1890 the church was restored again, and yet again in 1909.

Originally Sandringham Church can have had little or nothing to distinguish it from any other village church in Norfolk, but careful restoration, rich decoration and unique associations now combine to make it one of exceptional interest, and thousands of people flock from all over the world to visit it during the summer months.

As one enters by the south porch, it is worth looking up at the Guardian Angel holding a baby in the niche above the old doorway. In the porch there is a brass inscription to the effect that the church clock was given by King Edward VII and some friends as a memorial to Mr Christopher Sykes, who was a close friend of the King, and who died in 1898.

Continued on page 4

*

FACING PAGE: *The South Porch.*

RIGHT: *The carved stone angel over the entrance to the church is peculiar and unique. Why should an angel be carrying a baby? Was it once a Madonna, and the wings added at later date?*

3

Just inside the door is the inscription recording the restoration of the church in 1855 by Lady Harriette Cowper.

The organ is a fine one, made by John Walker and Co. It has three manuals, is electrically blown, and was the last gift of King Edward to the church in 1909, installed just seven months before he died.

The hatchments bearing the Royal Arms which one sees above the font at the west end of the church were placed on the outside of the railway coaches that bore the coffins of King George V and King George VI from Wolferton Station to London. Originally hatchments were affixed to the front of a dead man's house, bearing his coat of arms.

The nave is simple, with an English oak roof which was given in 1921 by King George V. On the walls are marble plaques to the memory of members of King Edward VII's family, inscribed with their names.

The pulpit is very unusual and was a gift to Queen Alexandra from Mr Rodman Wanamaker, presented on 1st December 1924, her 80th and last birthday.

The church being so small, a cleverly devised folding lectern was presented by King George VI in 1944. Made of oak, it is in keeping with the prayer-desk beside which it is placed, and it can be swung into position for the reading of the lessons and then folded back again.

The chancel arch is possibly a relic from an earlier church, though the responds and capitals belong to the 16th-century rebuilding.

The west window was placed in the church to the memory of H.R.H. The Duke of Clarence, K.G., elder son of King Edward, by his brother officers of the 10th Hussars, in which Regiment the Duke was a major.

Continued on page 8

*

LEFT: *This charming little Baptistry is at the base of the tower and contains an elegant Florentine marble font which was given by King Edward VII. It is surrounded by gilded angels. Above hang the colours of the Royal Norfolk Regiment.*

FACING PAGE: *This magnificent pulpit was presented to Queen Alexandra on the occasion of her 80th birthday in December 1924. The pulpit was actually dedicated in October 1926.*

THIS PAGE: *The pulpit is built of oak and panelled in solid silver with figure work in high relief, and a particularly striking central elongated figure of Our Lord. On either side are columns of tiny angels, then the four evangelists St Matthew, St Mark, St Luke and St John and, beyond these, scenes from our Lord's Ministry. They are the visit of the Wise Men; the coming of the Holy Spirit at Pentecost; the Feeding of the Five Thousand with the five loaves and two small fishes; and the Last Supper. The richly carved lower part of the pulpit fits into a bronze octagonal base which rests on a black marble plinth. At the foot of the* pulpit steps are two silver angels kneeling in prayer (illustrated on p. 11). The reading desk above is also in silver.*

* * *

FACING PAGE: *The south transept, added to the church in 1891. The window facing was given by Alfred, Duke of Edinburgh, to commemorate the 50th birthday of his brother King Edward VII (See page 9); the other window was presented at the same time by Queen Alexandra.*

as some are, if not unique, of extreme rarity.

Starting with the series in the south aisle window, from the east they represent:

St Erasmus, holding a crozier and a windlass. He was a Bishop, who suffered martyrdom by being disembowelled in A.D. 303.

St Agnes, Virgin and Martyr of Rome. She has a dagger in her neck and supports a lamb in her right hand. She suffered cruel torture and death in A.D. 304.

St Stephen, the first Christian Martyr. He holds stones in each hand, a reminder that he was stoned to death.

St Frances. She holds three darts or spears under her right arm, a scroll in her right hand and a large basket in her left which she is handing to a small female figure in a blue robe kneeling at her feet. She was a widow, a lady of noble character, who died in Rome in 1440 after founding a new religious order called the Collatines. It is said that there is no other representation of St Frances in England.

St Egedius (or *St Giles*), hermit and founder of the Abbey of St Gilles in the south of France. He lived in the early 8th century. He holds a crozier in his left hand, and a white fawn leaps up at him.

St Apollonia, holding a closed book in her left hand, forceps and a tooth in her right. She was a Virgin of Alexandria who suffered martyrdom in A.D. 250.

In a small compartment in the centre above is a nimbed female head with fair hair and a white rose. This concludes the series in the south window. Both here and on the north side the figures are arranged in pairs and facing each other.

In the north window, from the

★

THIS PAGE: *The north aisle window. The figures depicted in the upper lights of this window are (beginning from the east): St Leonard, St Vincent, St Margaret, St Brigina (or Bridget), St Ignatius of Antioch and St Michael.*

FACING PAGE: *The south transept window. It depicts the Draught of Fishes, the Walking on the Water and the Calming of the Storm, appropriate themes for a window presented by a Naval Officer. The window is captioned by the popular hymn 'For Those in Peril on the Sea'.*

The central figure represents St Edward, and it is rather unusual to see him portrayed with a moustache.

There is some glass of considerable interest in the nave, particularly the six figures of Saints in the upper lights of the north window, and six more in the corresponding situation in the window on the south side. These are worthy of some detailed description.

Charles Keyser, M.A., F.S.A., has identified and described this series of Saints as being of English glass and they probably belong to the date of the rebuilding of the church early in the 16th century, and are likely to be the work of a Norwich firm of glass painters, though possibly the windows are not in their original positions. They all have names and emblems which add to their interest east, the figures are:

St Leonard, holding a book and some fetters. Well known Saint and confessor who died in A.D. 546.

St Vincent, a little known Saint, holding a book and a large saw. He was a deacon of Saragossa and suffered a cruel martyrdom in A.D. 304.

St Margaret, clasping a cross and trampling on or emerging from a dark green dragon. A popular Saint and Virgin of Antioch, martyred in A.D. 306.

St Brigina (or *Bridget*), Abbess of Kildare, holding an open book and a pen with which she is writing. She flourished in the 6th century and was adopted Patroness of Ireland.

St Ignatius of Antioch, holding a crozier and probably a heart. Martyred about A.D. 107. He is another little known Saint and it is said that there is no other representation of him in England.

St Michael, the great Archangel and Captain of the Hosts of Heaven, pinning down a dragon with a cross.

In a small panel in the top of the window is a nimbed bearded head.

There are two more figures in the same series now inserted in the south wall of the porch. One is St Catherine of Alexandria, holding a wheel and a sword, who suffered cruel persecution, torture and death in A.D. 307.

The other is St Etheldreda, the saintly Queen who holds a crozier and a book. Founder and the first Abbess of the great Monastery of Ely, she died in A.D. 679, greatly venerated by all.

The only other glass in the church which is not modern is that in the centre main light on the north side. This is Flemish and is believed to have been removed from the church in the time of the Commonwealth. Although it is in a fragmentary condition it has been made up into patterns and is well worthy of notice. It was presented to the church by General Sir Dighton Probyn, V.C., in 1909 after having it arranged as a window by Sir Arthur Blomfield. One can distinguish the Judgement of Solomon, the Virgin and Child, St Giles and St Catherine, and a nimbed figure with carpenter's square. This glass probably dates from the early part of the 17th century.

After Sir Dighton Probyn's death in 1924, which occurred a year before that of the Queen whom he had

served so faithfully and so long, the sidelights of the window were filled with four scenes from the life of St George, bearing this inscription:

In memoriam, General the Right Honourable Sir Dighton MacNaghten Probyn, V.C., G.C.B., G.C.S.I., G.C.V.O., I.S.O., who for fifty-two years loyally served Their Majesties King Edward VII and Queen Alex- *andra, and who died at Sandringham, June 20th, 1924.*

'Thou wert the most courteous Knight that ever bare shield, the truest friend that ever bestrode horse, and the kindest man that ever struck with sword.'

This window was completed by those who were proud to share his friendship.

Continued on page 18

FACING PAGE: *The solid silver altar and reredos were presented to Queen Alexandra in 1911 by Mr Rodman Wanamaker, and they show Christ appearing to the Disciples, and the Royal Arms being supported by two angels. In the donor's words this gift 'is to commemorate the great service His Late Majesty rendered to the world by the manner in which he guided with great diplomacy the peaceful feelings of the English Nation'. It was Mr Wanamaker's wish that over this altar prayers should be constantly offered for the peace of all nations.*

ABOVE: *The enchanting little silver angels kneeling at the foot of the pulpit steps. The staircase and rail are of bronze with oak treads.*

RIGHT: *The coffin of His Late Majesty King George VI, resting in the chancel at Sandringham Church. Four game-keepers from the estate stand at the corners. They kept watch until the coffin was taken to Windsor.*

11

ABOVE: *Two of the delicately carved figures from the Sandringham 'Angel Choir' in the Sanctuary. Each of the fourteen angels plays a different musical instrument, and stands in a canopied niche. They form part of the memorial to King Edward VII, which was completed in 1920.*

FACING PAGE: *This view of the Chancel, looking towards the high altar, illustrates the wealth of glowing colours and variety of figures of saints, angels, kings and queens which abound here. It is true to say that Sandringham Church owes much to King Edward VII; not only was he a generous benefactor himself,* but much of the rich decoration has been added in his memory. There are two pews in the chancel, which are used only by the Royal Family and their Household and guests. Above are the delightful painted angel wall decorations, with a repeated design of the sacred monogram IHS.

FACING PAGE: *These figures are at each end of the two chancel pews and depict the Ministry of Angels recorded in the New Testament. At one end is (above left) the Archangel Gabriel and Our Lady of the Annunciation. For some unaccountable reason the Archangel has five fingers and a thumb on his right hand. At the other end (above right) is the Angel releasing St Peter from prison. On the opposite pew are (below left) Michael the Archangel defeating Lucifer and (below right) the Angel strengthening Our Lord in Gethsemane.*

ABOVE: *Pieces of the gold communion plate presented in 1927 by Rodman Wanamaker to King George V for Sandringham Church. The wafer box (below) is decorated with the twelve apostles round the sides; the ears of wheat form a cross on the lid.*

RIGHT: *This magnificent jewelled bible, given by Rodman Wanamaker, was made in America and weighs nearly two stone. The binding (above) is mounted with heavy silver-gilt scroll decorations set with over five hundred precious and semi-precious stones: emerald, sapphire, white opal, turquoise, garnet, amethyst, chrysoberyl, green tourmaline, pink topaz, pearls and topaz quartz.*

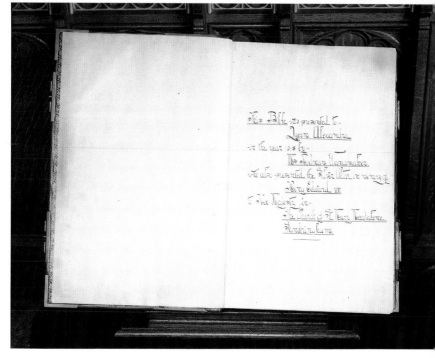

ABOVE: *The descriptions of these 16th-century south aisle windows are found on page 8.*

FACING PAGE: *A view from the richly decorated chancel to the nave. Above the choir stalls by the organ is a medallion of the Duke of Edinburgh, brother of King Edward VII, who brought the ancient font from Rhodes.*

The other windows have been put in by, or in memory of, friends of King Edward and Queen Alexandra, and have tablets underneath them recording this.

In marked contrast to the simplicity of the nave is the richly decorated chancel and sanctuary which glows with colour and splendour and gleams with silver and gold and precious stones. This is in some part due to the generosity of Mr Rodman Wanamaker, an American who was a great admirer of King Edward VII and of his work for the cause of peace. He presented the magnificent solid silver altar and reredos and bronze altar rails to Queen Alexandra on 6 May 1911, the first anniversary of the death of King Edward VII.

The centre of the reredos represents Christ appearing among His disciples with the words *Peace be unto you* underneath. At the foot of the reredos is the inscription: *To the Glory of God and in Memory of Edward VII the Peacemaker.*

The silver altar cross and candlesticks were the gifts of various members of King Edward's household and the altar lectern, also of silver, was given by King George V and Queen Mary in 1921.

The magnificent jewelled Bible in

★

LEFT: *The medallions of King Edward VII and Queen Alexandra* (top) *are in the chancel. Those of King George V and Queen Mary* (centre) *are above the pulpit and prayer desk. The inscriptions on the brass cross* (left) *on the chancel floor record the dates when the coffins of the Duke of Clarence, Queen Alexandra, King George V and King George VI rested here before being taken to Windsor. Tradition is that no one walks on the cross. The choir always divide as they pass it on entering and leaving the vestry. The plaque* (far left) *mounted on a nave pillar is of King George VI and was dedicated in the presence of the Royal Family on 30 December 1956.*

FACING PAGE: *This south side pew is used by Her Majesty The Queen and other members of the Royal Family during the annual New Year visit. Details of the interesting brass plates inserted into the pew book rest are described on page 20.*

the Sanctuary was presented by Mr Wanamaker in 1915. He also presented the silver processional cross, which was placed in the church by Queen Alexandra in 1920 in memory of the men from the Sandringham estate who died in the Great War of 1914–18. Owing to the beautiful detail and workmanship, the cross is extremely heavy and difficult to carry in a procession, though that is really its purpose.

The gentle colours of the east window blend perfectly with the gilded woodwork. It shows Our Lord on the Cross surrounded by prophets and kings. The angels' wings are copied from peacocks' feathers as are those of the eight painted angels on the walls of the chancel, which were given by King George V and Queen Mary in 1931.

The enrichment to the chancel and Sanctuary and the carved and painted decoration to the roof were given, with the east window, to the memory of King Edward VII by his wife, his children, his grandchildren, his household, his servants and the tenants and workers upon the estate.

Standing at the east end of the church one is surrounded by angels; there are eighty-four of them in the chancel and Sanctuary alone, and the carved angel choir is quite enchanting, each little figure so beautifully represented. The angel roof is characteristic of Norfolk. The decoration and embellishment of this memorial is unique, and in time will be a most interesting example of early 20th-century work.

Looking at the altar one sees a silver tablet on the wall on either side. The north side shows King Edward

kneeling at a faldstool with these words inscribed underneath:

To the beloved memory of Edward the Seventh of Great Britain and Ireland and of the British Dominion beyond the Seas, King, Defender of the Faith, Emperor of India, who for forty-seven years was a constant worshipper in this Church, and entered into Rest the 6th day of May, A.D. 1910. The Lord shall be unto thee an everlasting light, and thy God thy Glory.

On either side of this tablet are figures of St George of England and St David of Wales, and above are three kings—Edward the Confessor, the Lawgiver; Edward the First, Founder of Parliament; Edward III, Founder of the Order of the Garter.

Continued on page 20

Angels holding heraldic shields showing the Royal Arms follow the arch of the window up to the sacred monogram IHS which has adoring angels on either side. On the south side of the altar is a silver tablet with Queen Alexandra as the kneeling figure which bears this inscription:

To the hallowed memory of Queen Alexandra, wife of Edward VII, who for sixty-two years worshipped in this church, and entered into Rest the 20th day of November, A.D. 1925. Rest in Peace.

On either side of the tablet are figures of St Andrew of Scotland and St Patrick of Ireland, while above are three queens—Queen Bertha, the first Christian Queen in England, A.D. 597; St Margaret, Queen of Scotland; Queen Dagmar of Denmark.

The angels on this side hold shields showing the Arms of Queen Alexandra who, of course, came from Denmark; this is a happy and imaginative way of recording the alliance of the two Royal Houses.

The two pews in the chancel are used only by the Royal Family and their Household and guests. They are both entered by a small private vestry, The Queen and her family using the pew on the south side. It was here that King Edward and Queen Alexandra worshipped for so many years and there are three brass plates inserted into the book-rest, one saying that this seat 'was occupied by my beloved Husband from the year of our marriage, 1863, till 1910, when the Lord took him to Himself. Alexandra.'

The second plate records the death of the Duke of Clarence and says that 'this place was occupied for twenty-eight years by my darling Eddy, next to his ever sorrowing and loving Mother-dear, January 14th, 1892.' Queen Mary was betrothed to the Duke of Clarence, who was the elder son of King Edward and Queen Alexandra. After the Duke's death she married his younger brother, the then Duke of York who became King George V.

When his mother died, King George V had the third brass plate inserted

with the words 'My beloved Mother occupied this seat for sixty-two years

Continued on page 22

★

ABOVE (left): *This silver cross, Spanish in origin and over 460 years old, has on one side the figure of our Lord on the Cross and on the reverse side St Andrew.*

ABOVE (right): *The organ has a frontage of spotted metal pipes, in a case of carved oak, made to the design of Arthur Bloomfield Esq., M.A., F.R.I.B.A. There are three manuals with 25 speaking stops. The Swell and Choir are enclosed with balanced crescendo pedals. The action is tubular-pneumatic. See also the note on page 4.*

FACING PAGE: *The angel wall decoration on the south side of the church. The silver tablet is dedicated to Queen Alexandra. It is set into an elaborate Gothic design which includes figures of three queens: Bertha, first Christian queen in England; Margaret of Scotland and Dagmar of Denmark.*

from 1863 to 1925, next to her sorrowing son, George, R.I.'

Behind the Royal pew are two windows, one in memory of the baby Prince Alexander who lived only for one day in this world in 1871, and the other in memory of Lieut.-Colonel Grey, equerry to H.R.H. The Prince of Wales, by whom the window was presented in 1878.

The carved figures on the Royal pews depict the Ministry of Angels. It will be seen that the Angel Gabriel has been given an extra finger.

In the corner of the Royal pew there is a lovely crystal and silver-gilt cross set in a canopied niche. This was given by Sir Dighton Probyn, V.C., after King Edward died, and the inscription reveals his devotion to his King and Queen.

King Edward VII and Queen Alexandra. A thank offering to Almighty God, placed in Sandringham church by one whose joy it was to serve his King and Queen, whose comfort now

to serve his Queen.
        D. M. Probyn, 1911.

Nearby, at the west end of the Royal pew, is a very beautiful aluminium and ivory statuette of St George.

The Duke of Clarence, Queen Alexandra, King George V and King George VI all died at Sandringham, and let into the marble floor of the chancel is a brass cross above which their coffins rested before going to Windsor for burial. Owing to the thousands of visitors to this little church every year, the chancel floor has to be kept covered on week-days or it would be scratched and damaged by so many footsteps.

In the vestry there is a Jacobean carved oak chest with *Sainte Marie Magdaelene* 1625 inscribed on it. This is the only sign or mention in the church of the Patron Saint. It is a very fine old chest which is believed to have originally belonged here.

At the west end of the church, outside the tower, is a most unusual

and interesting ancient Greek font. This was brought from the Island of Rhodes in 1886 by the Duke of Edinburgh for his brother, then Prince of Wales, and is very probably of the 9th century.

There is a Greek inscription around the upper rim which, translated, reads: 'In the treasureship of Cyriacus, a deacon, and Calvinus (the) humble, this work was executed: and may the Lord preserve those that erect it. Amen.'

There can be no doubt that the
Continued on page 24

★

ABOVE: *The Queen and the Royal Family enter the church through this door.*

FACING PAGE: *Sandringham is a parish church and therefore is open to all who wish to worship. The congregation is composed of those who belong to the Sandringham group of parishes together with the many visitors on holiday in the area.*

object itself is a marble font. There are two other known examples, one a font of the 4th century, excavated at Tyre, which is almost exactly the same shape, though larger; and one of marble in the Museum of Antiquities at Istanbul. In general, however, fonts in the western sense were not used in the east; there was, instead, more often a baptistry attached to the larger churches and a basin of some sort occupied its centre. The most complete example of such a structure is the Baptistry of the Orthodox Church at Ravenna, and the Sandringham font no doubt originally occupied the centre of a similar though smaller edifice.

The thoughts of people all over the world turn towards Sandringham after Christmas when The Queen arrives. Here it is that she and her family can be free from the glare of public life and enjoy themselves in peace—walking, shooting, riding, going to church and wandering freely through the woods and fields enjoying the heather, the trees and the sea.

When King Edward VII, then Prince of Wales, bought the estate in 1862, it consisted of 8,000 acres; now it has 20,000. Even when rebuilt Sandringham House was not big enough to accommodate the many guests whom His Royal Highness delighted to entertain, and so York

Cottage was built in the grounds.

'Dear old Sandringham,' said King George V, 'the place I love better than anywhere in the world.' He and Queen Mary made York Cottage their home at Sandringham until the death of Queen Alexandra in 1925. King George VI was born at York Cottage, baptised in Sandringham Church and died at Sandringham House.

The House was rebuilt by King Edward VII in brick in modified Elizabethan style. It was finished in 1870, and in 1892 was enlarged in the local carrstone. Today it is surrounded by lawns, the flower beds having been drastically reduced.

The home farms, consisting of some 3,000 acres, are mixed arable and beef farming and are run most scientifically and productively. Cattle are sent to agricultural shows all over Britain, and win many prizes.

About 2,000 acres of woodland are being extensively re-afforested, their natural cover helping to make Sandringham one of the greatest sporting estates in the country. All the parkland is grazed with cattle and the produce from the gardens is sent to Buckingham Palace and for sale to various markets. The remaining 15,000 acres of the estate are let to tenant farmers.

The Queen's Stud is at Sandringham and Wolferton. Mares are brought from all over the country and give

birth to their delightful little foals here.

Here, too, is the little station which has been seen in the past (but now no longer) so many Royal arrivals and departures, gay with flowers in the spring and summer, and with fir trees and coloured lights to decorate the platforms at Christmas.

The Church of St Mary Magdalene is perfectly situated on the Royal estate. It is backed by trees, is on the highest point in the park, and from it one looks across the beautifully kept churchyard with its Georgian tombstones to the rolling parkland and woods. The Rectory is on one side and on the other side is an avenue of Scots pines leading to Sandringham House. When the Royal Family come to church they enter the churchyard through a lychgate and pass the graves of the two little Princes, Alexander, the tiny son of King Edward and Queen Alexandra, and John, fifth son of King George V and Queen Mary.

Sunday by Sunday the parish church ministers the Word and Sacraments to the people of the estate. Apart from the privilege of having the Royal family in church when they are in residence, Sandringham is no different from any other country parish. The Rector of Sandringham is Domestic Chaplain to The Queen. He also has seven other parishes, known as the Sandringham Group of Eight Parishes, for which he and another priest are responsible. The little church itself is enriched with loving memories of a united family, faithful in their worship and constant in their affection for one another. Today the position of the Throne is as strong as ever, not least because of the example set by the Royal family in their religion and family life.

*

ABOVE: *The Greek font, which is outside the tower at the west end of the church. It was brought from Rhodes and is considered to be about eleven hundred years old.*

*

ACKNOWLEDGMENTS
All the photographs in this book were taken by Angelo Hornak, with the exception of the following: pp. i cover, 1, 4, 8, 9, 12, 13, 21 by C. J. Nicholas, A.I.I.P.; p. 11 (below) by Thomson Newspapers Ltd; pp. 15 (above left), 18 by A. F. Kersting, A.I.I.P., F.R.P.S.; pp. 17, 20 (left) by S. W. Newbery, Hon. F.I.I.P., F.R.P.S.

SBN 85372 065 7